Prayer is My Superpower

Discovering and Activating the
Power of Prayer for Black Boys

By: Zaccheus L. Moss

JT PUBLISHING HOUSE

Prayer Is My Superpower
Copyright © 2025 by Zaccheus Moss

Names: Moss, Zaccheus.
Title: Prayer/ Zaccheus Moss.
Summary: "Prayer Is My Superpower follows Jackson, a young boy who embarks on a journey to understand and develop his ability to pray. Inspired by a conversation with a new friend at church, Jackson learns that prayer is a powerful tool—one that requires no cape or mask but can help him overcome challenges."-- Provided by author.

Identifiers: ISBN 978-1-954624-23-8 (paperback) | ISBN 978-1-954624-24-5 (ebook)
Subjects: BISAC: Children's / Teenage general interest: Religious texts, prayers and devotional material
Library of Congress Control Number: 2025907469

Published by JT Publishing, Spartanburg, South Carolina
www.jtpublishinghouse.com

Printed in the United States of America

DEDICATION

This book is dedicated to black boys who face difficulty, to no fault of their own. Know, that our Heavenly Father desires a relationship with you through prayer. Activate your super-power!

TABLE OF CONTENTS

PRAYER OF ENCOURAGEMENT

In Ephesians 3:14-20 (NKJV), bib-lical teacher and superhero Paul writes:

For this reason, I bow my knees to the Father of our Lord Jesus Christ, from whom the whole fam-ily in heaven and earth is named, that He would grant you, accord-ing to the riches of His glory, to be strengthened with might through His Spirit in the inner man, that Christ may dwell in your hearts through faith; that you, being rooted and grounded in love, may be able to comprehend with all the saints what is the width and length and depth and height—to know the love of Christ which passes knowledge; that you may be filled with all the fullness of God.

Now to Him who is able to do exceedingly abundantly above all that we ask or think, according to the power that works in us, to Him be glory in the church by Christ Jesus to all generations, forever and ever. Amen.

It's time to discover and activate the superpower of prayer in your life.

INTRODUCTION

Black Panther, Batman, Superman, Flash, Aquaman, Ironman, Captain America, Thor, Spiderman, The Incredible Hulk, and Wolverine are well-known superheroes. We are familiar with their special abilities and unique superpowers. We marvel at their ability to face challenges from their enemy, cheer them during battles, and stand proud when they are victorious.

Do you realize that you, too, are a superhero?

Yes, you.

No matter what your brother, sister, or even a bully might say, you have a superpower within you.

Don't worry; no fancy suit, cape, or mask is needed to discover or activate your superpower.

How do I know? Because your superpower is prayer!

There is no situation or obstacle where prayer will not offer the help that is needed.

As you read Jackson's story, you will be introduced to the different prayers he prayed as he learned how to pray. You will also see how he prayed for things that mattered to him, prayed for his future, and used various tools to strengthen his prayer life.

You can use the prayers Jackson prayed for your personal prayer time too. In your life, there are challenges you will face, especially as a young black boy.

Think of this book as your secret weapon to defeat those obstacles and see yourself raising your hands as a WINNER!

Are you ready?

Repeat after me, "Prayer is my superpower!"

JACKSON'S SUPERPOWER

Prayer Is My Superpower

DISCOVERING THE SUPERPOWER

On Sunday morning, like every Sunday morning, Jackson's mother woke him up at the same time for church service, a routine he'd grown to expect.

He brushed his teeth and put on the clothes his mother picked out for him—pants, shoes, and a tie. Jackson looked forward to seeing his family and friends at church, but he was most excited about eating his favorite meal—fried chicken—afterward.

As they arrived to church,

Prayer Is My Superpower

Jackson greeted everyone with a big smile. However, he noticed a young man he didn't know, who appeared to be a few years older than him, praying aloud.

The image and sound of the young man praying stuck with Jackson throughout the service, so he approached the young man afterward to introduce himself.

"What's up, man? That was a good message today on prayer. I don't know if I've ever heard that prayer is a superpower," said Jackson.

"Yeah, it was good. The preacher today is my dad."

"Oh wow, I'm Jackson."

"What's up, Jackson! I'm William," he replied.

Amazed, Jackson and William continued to talk. Jackson asked more and more questions about prayer.

Throughout the conversation, Jackson imagined himself possessing the superpower of prayer.

Not long after that conversation, Jackson found himself on a journey to discover how he could learn to develop and use the superpower of prayer, and he knew exactly where to start.

Prayer Is My Superpower

TEACH ME HOW TO PRAY

Jackson wanted to learn how to pray, so he talked with his parents. They shared different things about prayer, and he understood most of what they shared, but not everything.

He decided to talk with his grandparents. He believed they knew how to help unlock the superpower of prayer.

They lovingly talked with him and told him to get in a quiet place and just talk to God like you are talking to a friend.

Prayer Is My Superpower

"Talk to God like I'm talking to a friend?" Jackson questioned.

"Yes, just like a friend," his grandparents shared.

Jackson became quite curious and excited, but he was still not entirely convinced that simply talking to God like a friend would activate the superpower of prayer.

The following Sunday, he asked Reverend Craig, "How do I activate the superpower of prayer?"

The preacher smiled at Jackson and said, "Son, it begins with a relationship. Before you can talk to anyone, you must be in some form of relationship. You can't be strangers."

Jackson nodded.

"Have you decided to join the family of God?" asked Reverend Craig.

Jackson looked confused.

"Joining the family of God begins with confessing you have done things that you know were not right, believing Jesus died on the cross for those things, was raised three days later from the dead, and is alive in Heaven today with God. Then, you choose to be baptized to show that you are alive in Christ Jesus.

But, when you can say you believe what Jesus Christ did for you on the cross, without any doubt in your heart, you are no longer a stranger to

Prayer Is My Superpower

God.

The desire to communicate with God activates prayer, but it only becomes your superpower when you have a relationship with God. No matter what circumstance you find yourself in, the power of prayer is within you, and God is waiting to activate it right now," shared Reverend Craig.

Jackson felt his heart beating and palms sweating, but he was not anxious. He felt peaceful excitement. He believed with all his hear that Jesus died on the cross for him and rose again.

Reverend Craig could see something happening inside of Jackson, so he waited a few moments.

"Jackson," said Reverend Craig, "what you are feeling is the beginning of your superpower of prayer being activated."

"Can we pray?" asked Jackson.

Overwhelmed by Jackson's request, Reverend Craig began to pray and thank God for Jackson. He prayed that Jackson always remembered that moment and the superpower of prayer as long as he lived.

Jackson thanked Reverend Craig and asked if he could pray for him.

A bit timid, Jackson began to pray, "God thank you for Reverend Craig. Take care of his health and his family, and keep him encouraged as he preaches to us your people. Amen."

Reverend Craig was overjoyed. Tears flowed down his face. He knew his prayers were answered, and Jackson, a young boy, was used as his hero.

"Jackson, continue praying. Talk to God every day, and you will watch Him change your life," said Reverend Craig.

Jackson agreed to pray daily.

JACKSON LEARNS TO PRAY

Prayer Is My Superpower

IT'S JUST THE BEGINNING

For the first time, Jackson prayed by himself. He knew he wanted to learn about prayer, and felt that the best thing to do was start. He closed his eyes and prayed.

> God, I am just beginning a relationship with you, and I need to figure out where to start. You are called many names by those older than me. Of course, I have heard of you being called God, but I've also heard you called Father in the Lord's Prayer.

If you do not mind, I will call you Father.

Thank you for not dismissing my youth and not judging me because of how I look. You love me just as I am.

I want to talk to you about everything.

Jackson knew he needed a life of prayer, and he was excited to begin. Amen.

MY NEW PRAYER LIFE

With his heart full of hope, Jackson began to pray:

> Father, I have been taught that you hear and answer prayers. As I begin this journey, I know that you know everything, have all power, and you are everywhere.
>
> My prayer is simple today as I begin this journey.
>
> Each day, I want to learn more about you and how to pray.

Prayer Is My Superpower

Help me God to discover and activate the power of prayer that is within me. Help me to not just pray for myself but teach me to pray for others.

Thank you for this time, and thank you for my family, Amen.

Jackson was grateful that he was no longer a stranger to God and he was continuing to develop his relationship with Him.

THANKSGIVING

As Jackson embraced the start of a new day, he was filled with gratitude. He bowed his head and prayed:

Father, thank you for waking me up today. Thank you for my family and my friends.

Thank you forfood, clothing, and shelter. I am grateful for you allowing me to taste, smell, talk, hear, see, run, walk, and think.

I know there are times that I take things for granted, but I am aware that you are constantly working on my behalf.

As I go throughout today, help me remain thankful for the simple things in life and allow me to serve as an example to others. Father, as you have given me the gift of life, I will not miss this opportunity to thank you.

Amen.

Jackson was ready to take on the world!

PROTECTION

Jackson realized that prayer is a way to talk to God about anything so he prayed for protection.

Father, I start today with you on my mind. I praise you, God, because you love me enough to protect my family, friends, and me. While I was sleeping last night, you sent your angels to watch over me. Thank you!

As I go through this day, help me be an example to others and have faith and trust in you, in Jesus'

Prayer Is My Superpower

name, Amen.

MORNING PRAYER

Jackson was building muscle in prayer and started each day with talking to God.

Father, as I begin this day, I seek you early so I can be filled with the strength I need for the day ahead. Just as food is needed to survive, help me be nourished by your word and not starve myself from what is essential.

Father, give me a heart that seeks your word, so I can have a plan for success.

Thank you, Father, for loving me and drawing me closer to you, especially in my youth. I will stay connected to you throughout my life.

Amen.

Jackson knew he could talk to God any time during the day, and knowing God always heard him gave him peace.

FUEL DURING THE DAY

As Jackson went about his day, he found himself without the energy to perform at his best. He realized that just as cars require fuel to operate, he needed fuel for his day also. As Jackson learned how to pray, he also learned to trust that God hears and responds when we pray.

Jackson knew his energy to get through his day well would come from spending time in prayer.

There at school, Jackson closed his eyes and prayed.

Prayer Is My Superpower

Father, today, I have an increased appreciation for learning. Give me the fuel I need to do my best work academically without the weight of frustration and uncertainty.

Motivate me and cause me to soar academically without the need for popularity and the distractions of peer pressure.

Father, take away bullying, violence, drugs, suicide, and failure. Thank you for allowing me to learn freely without any inhibitions or interruptions and for giving me the energy to focus.

Amen.

END OF THE DAY PRAYER

After a busy day, Jackson took a moment to pray before going to bed:

Father, thank you for being with me today. As this day comes to an end, I want to take a moment to thank you for keeping me safe from things I didn't even know could hurt me. I'm thankful that I wasn't in a dangerous situation, that I didn't get hurt, and that I wasn't involved in something bad by mistake.

Thank you, Father, for watching

over my parents, siblings, relatives, and friends.

I'm thankful for everything you've done for me, even the things I forget to appreciate.

Thank you for tomorrow and the chance it brings for me to do what I'm meant to do. Thank you for giving me peace and rest tonight, and for letting me wake up tomorrow feeling refreshed.

Amen.

JACKSON PRAYS ABOUT HIS LIFE

Prayer Is My Superpower

PEACE

The growth and development of Jackson's prayer life made him more and more comfortable talking to God. He realized he could be honest with God and tell Him anything.

Jackson knew he needed peace of mind to make it through the day without distractions. He stopped to pray.

Father, I'm taking a moment right now to focus on you and put everything else aside.

Prayer Is My Superpower

With my TV off, my game system quiet, and my AirPods down, I want to really connect with you.

There have been times when I've felt overwhelmed and didn't know how to deal with everything. I've tried to find answers from friends and family, but it just didn't feel like enough.

With all the choices I have to make, the peer pressure I'm facing, and the worries that keep me up, I'm asking for your peace— something beyond what I can understand. I know if I keep my mind on you, you'll keep me in perfect peace.

Thank you for the blessings today

and for the peace that's coming my way.

Amen.

After Jackson prayed, he felt better and sensed God's peace. His heart was filled with gratitude.

Prayer Is My Superpower

CONFIDENCE

Jackson heard some hurtful words that made him feel bad about himself. The sting of those words was real, but instead of letting it get to him, Jackson did what he knew would help, he prayed.

Thank you, Father, for reminding me that I am fearfully and wonderfully made. Not only that, but you created me in your image and likeness. I can be confident knowing that you, God, are great; therefore, I am great. Help me confidently walk in your word, which tells me I am to be on top and not on the bottom. God, I give praise that you know the plans you have for me and the expected outcome you have for my life. When my confidence begins to shrink and diminish, bring to my mind that I am your son, and you are well pleased in Jesus' name, Amen.

FRIENDSHIPS

Jackson learned the hard way that sometimes our friends can get us into trouble, and that we can get our friends into trouble as well.

Overall, he realized who we choose to become friends with is a big deal and really matters.

Jackson prayed to be the kind of friend that brings out the best in others and that his friends do the same. As Jackson took a moment to pray:

Prayer Is My Superpower

Father, thank you for this new day of life. Thank you for the opportunity to enjoy the fruit of this day.

Thank you for all the blessings of previous days and days to come. I am beginning to understand that friendships are important in my life.

Some friendships have led me to make good decisions, but some have led me to get into trouble.

Father, I want to have friendships in school and be a part of sports teams, but I need your help to make the right choices.

Please help me be the leader of my friends. Let our choices be good ones that keep us out of trouble with our parents, teachers, coaches, and adults.

Father, give me the courage to speak up when my friends suggest things I know are wrong.

Give me the confidence to stand firm in what I have been taught and the strength to hold true to my beliefs. Amen.

Prayer Is My Superpower

ACADEMICS

Jackson desired to excel academically, but some things he didn't quite understand, and he didn't want to ask the teacher for help. Jackson doesn't want his friends or other students to laugh. So Jackson deccides to get by himself at home and prays.

As Jackson started his day, he prayed:

Father, I'm thankful for this new day. I appreciate my teachers, parents, and everyone who's pushing me to do well. Please help me understand what I'm learning today and give me the courage to ask questions when I don't get something.

God, take away any fear of asking what others might think is a "dumb" question.

Help me stay focused during class and show respect to my teachers, my classmates, and myself through what I say and do.

Amen.

SPORTS

Jackson was frustrated after his team lost the championship game. He let his anger take over and didn't show good sportsmanship. He realized he had focused too much on the one loss and not enough on the ten wins that were actually a blessing.

He realized that in order to show true sportsmanship he would have to ask God for help.

Father, I know you created everything, including me, and I'm grateful for that. I love playing sports with my friends, and I ask that you protect me during every practice and game.

I want to win, God, but please teach me to have discipline, good sportsmanship, and respect for others whether we win or lose.

Help me remember that even though I put a lot of time and energy into sports, I need to make time for you too.

Forgive me for the times I've forgotten about you or acted out of character.

Thank you for the opportunity to be a part of these teams.

Amen.

BEING VALUABLE AND UNIQUE

Sometimes at school, Jackson felt left out of the group. The feeling of being isolated started to weigh on him, and he felt a little dread when it came to school.

Jackson decided to pause, pray, and talk to God about his feelings.

Father, today I praise you as my King, my protector, my provider, and the source of all the good things in my life.

Prayer Is My Superpower

I ask that you protect me from negative thoughts and from people who might try to bring me down.

Help me appreciate how unique I am and to see my value. Teach me to focus on success, determination and perseverance, and to block out the negative voices that try to distract me.

Help me recognize my own worth and understand how valuable others are too.

Amen.

SUCCESS

Being successful mattered to Jackson. He wanted to experience success at school and at home every day. Jackson knew God heard and answered his prayers, so he paused to pray.

Father, cause my dreams of success to become a reality. I ask you to hear my cries for affirmation in moments of painful silence. Lead me toward experiences in books that feed my appetite for adventure without the risk of harm.

Father, make sure that my school is safe and serves as a launching pad for success. Help me avoid the mistakes of my parents that could leave permanent marks as barriers to future success.

I pray for blessings of peace, patience, wisdom, and innovation for my teachers. I pray they create lesson plans that bring out the best in me.

Amen.

MALE ROLE MODELS

On his way home from school, Jackson saw an interaction between an older male and a young boy.

He saw the joy on the young boy's face, and it made him appreciate the male role models in his life. He understood that having people in your corner to show you and tell you right from wrong was important.

As Jackson continued walking, he prayed.

Father, thank you for placing male

role models in my life and giving me examples I can follow.

Thank you for fathers, uncles, grandfathers, brothers, teachers, and pastors that I can see in the community for guidance. Give me the wisdom to avoid influences that lead to a path you never intended for me to follow.

Father, allow my thoughts to connect to having the best life. Let my hands not touch things that bring death or destruction. Guard my eyes against negative images that can impact my life now or in the future. Guide my feet so that my steps are ordered and draw me closer to you.

Amen.

Jackson was grateful for the relationships he had and realized the impact they had on his identity.

Prayer Is My Superpower

IDENTITY

As Jackson considered who he was destined to become, he wanted to talk to God about his identity. He was aware that people can say a lot of things about you, but what really matters is how God sees you and allows you to see yourself.

God, as I learn more about you, I realize there's so much more to discover. I've seen my parents, grandparents, and others trust you, and I want to trust you too. Help me to know you as my Creator. I pray that you show me who

I am and who you made me to be.

Father, I know you understand the fun things I like, but you also know what makes me sad, hurts my feelings, and makes me feel scared. When others don't think much of me, help me remember that you see the best in me.

I'm thankful that even when I mess up, you still love me. Help me to see myself the way you see me.

Amen.

Jackson recognized how important his identity was to God and how much God cares about every detail of who we are.

JACKSON PRAYS FOR HIS FUTURE

Prayer Is My Superpower

PERSONAL PRAYER

The future was important to Jackson. He knew trusting God was the best option to make sure his life was on track now and later. He paused to pray.

Father, I thank you for making me a Black boy.

I admit, Father, that sometimes fear rises in me, especially when I see tragedies happening to boys who look like me.

Give me the courage and strength

I need every day to live without fear.

Father, as you walk with me through the challenges I face, I will not let fear take over. Instead, I will pause, pray, and move forward knowing you don't give me a spirit of fear but empower me with love and clear thinking. Walk with me in Jesus's name, Amen.

DISCIPLINE

While growing in prayer, Jackson realized there were times when he spent less time with God and felt distracted by life. He chose to shut down the distractions and take time to pray. Discipline to focus was what he needed to ask God for during prayer.

Father, as this day unfolds, I place my life completely in your hands. Thank you for giving me the tools I need for success.

Please help me not to rebel against my parents' wisdom and instructions because I know they only want the best for me.

Help me stay focused on being successful and not give in to distractions. Keep me focused on reaching my goals and showing the character traits that lead to success.

Help me to stay committed to my time with you because success ultimately comes from you. I thank you for the discipline to finish and stay the course according to your plan for my life.

Amen.

I AM NOT ALONE

As Jackson reflected on life's challenges and blessings, he was grateful that he did not have to navigate life without God. He closed his eyes and prayed:

Father, I come to you today knowing that every day is not filled with the best of life. There are moments when I feel like no one understands me.

Hear my heart today, and if I feel alone, reveal yourself to me. I know you have always had my best interests in mind and have plans for a great future of success.

You have not left me by myself. My parents trust you and so do I. I know you will not abandon me. Wipe my tears in lonely moments.

Father, lift my head in hard times and use others to encourage me when I need it.

Help me to inspire others as well, Father.

Amen.

As Jackson began to see those less fortunate than himself, he realized he had more than enough to be thankful for and God had not and would not ever leave him alone.

UPLIFTING PRAYER

Wanting guidance, Jackson bowed his head and prayed. He knew God would hear and encourage his heart about the future.

Our Father who art in Heaven, holy is your name.

Father, I come to you today knowing there will be a time I encounter peer pressure to fit into the "in crowd."

Give me the confidence to love the skin that you blessed me with, treasure the life I have, and the ability to appreciate all my blessings.

Please help me remember I am a loved son of the King.

Amen.

DIRECTION

Before he started his day, Jackson prayed:

Father, during difficult moments, hear my voice and respond with love. When I don't know what to do next, I will turn to you, God, because I know you will give me clear directions.

When I face decisions that seem like the best choice, but later I realize the outcome wasn't what I expected because it was only about what I wanted—not about pleasing you—help me to recognize that.

Help me acknowledge you and listen to your guidance when I make decisions. Teach me to obey your directions and not think I know everything.

I know your guidance also comes through my parents, so if I lose my way, help me to turn back and not be too proud to ask for help. Thank you for the gift of prayer because I can always come to you no matter what!

Amen.

JACKSON'S PRAYER TOOLS

Prayer Is My Superpower

PRAYER TOOLS

Jackson's prayer life didn't stop. He continued to pray and seek God for guidance for his life. He used different prayer tools to ensure he maintained an active life of prayer.

As you're building your prayer time with God, you can use Jackson's tools to support your prayer time. No matter what, don't stop praying to God and know you are loved by our Heavenly Father and He always hears you.

Prayer Is My Superpower

5 PRAYER TOOLS

- T.A.C.O.S.

- A.C.T.S.

- H.E.A.R.T.

- H.E.A.R.

- 5 FINGER PRAYER MODEL

T.A.C.O.S.

- Thanksgiving-Thanking God for what He has done

- Adoration-Adoring God for who He is

Prayer Is My Superpower

- Confession-Confessing what you have done wrong

- Others-Praying for others

- Self-Praying for yourself

A.C.T.S.

- Admire God for his greatness

- Conversation with God about wrong acts

- Thanking God for his acts

- Submitting prayers for yourself and others

P.R.A.Y.

- Praise God for who you know him to be

- Repent for what you did wrong

- Ask God for help

- Yield your way to God's way

H.E.A.R.T.

- Honor God with praise

- Examine your life for wrongdoing

- Ask God for help for yourself

- Request help from God for others

- Thank God

H.E.A.R.

- Honor God

- Examine yourself for disobedience

Prayer Is My Superpower

- Ask for God's help and forgiveness

- Repent with thanks and change

5 FINGER PRAYER GUIDE

This five-finger guide helps us focus our prayers.

1. **Thumb.** Our thumb is closest to us and reminds us to pray for our family and loved ones.

2. **Index finger.** Our index finger is related to those who direct, teach, and heal us.

3. **Middle finger.** Our middle finger is the longest and focuses on those in government, such as the president, Supreme Court, Congress, and governors.

4. **Ring finger.** Our fourth finger, the ring finger, is our weakest finger and reminds us to pray for those less fortunate than us and those who deal

with sickness.

5. **Pinky finger.** Our pinky finger ensures that we remember to pray for ourselves after we have prayed for others. In praying for others, we will discover the area(s) of our need.

THE ABC PLAN

I know you have seen loved ones and friends die, some due to tragedies, sickness, or age. Have you thought about whether they are spending eternity in heaven or hell?

Do you know whether you will be spending eternity in heaven or hell?

Does knowing your current standing with eternity cause fear?

I have good news; you don't have to be unclear about where you will spend eternity. The ABC Plan can help you get clear quickly.

A-Accept the Lord Jesus as your Savior from your sins.

B-Believe that God raised Jesus from the

dead three days after dying on the cross.

C-Confess that you have sinned, and you will be saved.

Once you follow the ABC Plan, you will, without a doubt, spend eternity in heaven. However, many people do not decide to give their lives to Christ before it is too late.

Will you pray with me?

Father, I know I am young and think I have many years left to live, but I have seen young and older people die around me. Father, I want to be ready to spend eternity with you.

I confess my sins to you, God, and thank you for your forgiveness.

I believe you raised your son, Jesus,

from the tomb after dying on the cross for me. Father, I wholeheartedly accept you as my Lord and Savior this day, Amen.

Welcome to God's family and know that your destination is heaven. Do not allow those friends around you to remain unsure of their eternal home when you hold the key. Walk them through the ABC Plan.

Prayer Is My Superpower

SCRIPTURES
TO READ AND REMEMBER

The Lord's Prayer

"Our Father in heaven, we pray that your name will always be kept holy. We pray that your kingdom will come—that what you want will be done here on earth, the same as in heaven.

Give us the food we need for today. Forgive our sins, just as we have forgiven those who did wrong to us. Don't let us be tempted, but save us from the Evil One" (Matthew 6:9-13, EASY).

Prayer Is My Superpower

GOD IS A CARING PROVIDER

Psalms 23:1: "The Lord is my shepherd; I shall not want" (NKJV).

ULTIMATE GIFT OF LOVE-JESUS

John 3:16: "For God so loved the world that He gave His only begotten Son, that whoever believes in Him should not perish but have everlasting life" (NKJV).

BE AND THINK DIFFERENTLY

Romans 12:2: "Do not become like the people who belong to this world. But let God completely change the way that you think, so that you live differently. Then you will understand what God wants you to do. You will know what is good. You will know what pleases God. You will know what is completely right" (EASY).

FAITH, TRUST, AND HOPE

Hebrews 11:1: "This is what it means to trust God: We will be sure about the things that we hope for. We will be sure in our minds about things that we cannot even see" (EASY).

IDENTITY OF GREATNESS

1 John 4:4: "You are of God, little children, and have overcome them, because He who is in you is greater than he who is in the world" (NKJV).

Ephesians 3:20: "Now to Him who is able, to do exceedingly abundantly above all that we ask or think, according to the power that works in us"

(NKJV).

Philippians 4:13: "I can do all things through Christ who strengthens me" (NKJV).

DON'T WORRY. PRAY

Philippians 4:6-7: "Do not worry about anything. Instead, pray to God about everything. Ask him to help you with the things that you need. And thank him for his help. If you do that, God will give you peace in your minds. That peace is so great that nobody can completely understand it. You will not worry or be afraid, because you belong to Christ Jesus" (EASY).

REJOICE. PRAY. GIVE THANKS

1 Thessalonians 5:16-18: "Rejoice always, pray without ceasing, give thanks in all circumstances; for this is the will of God in Christ Jesus for you" (ESV).

DEVELOP A HABIT OF PRAISE

Psalms 34:1: "I will bless the Lord at all times; His praise shall continually be in my mouth" (NKJV).

GOD IS OUR GPS

Proverbs 3:5-6: "Trust in the LORD with all thine heart; And lean not unto thine own understanding. In all thy ways acknowledge him, And he shall direct thy paths" (KJV).

NO REASON TO FEAR: GOD IS WITH

US

Joshua 1:9: "Remember that I have told you this: Be strong and do not be afraid. Do not be weak, but be brave" (EASY).

WAIT: GOD'S HELP IS ON THE WAY

Psalms 27:14: "Wait for the Lord to help you! Be strong and brave. Yes, wait for the Lord to help you" (EASY).

GOD IS GOOD ALL THE TIME

1 Chronicles 16:34: "Oh, give thanks to the Lord, for He is good! For His mercy endures forever" (NKJV).

GOD IS AN ON TIME GOD

Isaiah 65:24: "And it shall come to pass, that before they call, I will answer; and while they are yet speaking, I will hear" (KJV).

There is power in the words we speak. Our words have within them the necessary power to build up or to tear down.

The words that we speak daily strengthen us for all the villains, enemies, challenges and obstacles that come against us. To arm us in our fight, use these tools. These super power affirmations will prove helpful when spoken daily and partnered with daily prayers.

Prayer Is My Superpower

SUPERPOWER AFFIRMATIONS

Prayer is my superpower! God is within me. God hears me.

Prayer is my superpower! God is within me. God hears me. God gives me purpose.

Prayer is my superpower! God is within me. God hears me. God removes my fear.

Prayer is my superpower! God is within me. God hears me. God gives me identity.

Prayer is my superpower! God is within me. God hears me. God removes my guilt.

Prayer Is My Superpower

Prayer is my superpower! God is within me. God hears me. God gives me faith.

Prayer is my superpower! God is within me. God hears me. God gives me a family.

Prayer is my superpower! God is within me. God hears me. God gives me friends.

Prayer is my superpower! God is within me. God hears me. God gives me talents.

Prayer is my superpower! God is within me. God hears me. God teaches me.

Prayer is my superpower! God is within me. God hears me. God gives me understanding.

Prayer is my superpower! God is within me. God hears me. God protects me.

Prayer is my superpower! God is within me. God hears me. God is my guide.

Prayer is my superpower! God is within me. God hears me. God loves me.

Prayer is my superpower! God is within me. God hears me. God is my friend.

Prayer is my superpower! God is within me. God hears me. God is my healer.

Prayer Is My Superpower

Prayer is my superpower! God is within me. God hears me. God gave Jesus to me.

Prayer is my superpower! God is within me. God hears me. God gives me peace.

Prayer is my superpower! God is within me. God hears me. God gives me joy.

Prayer is my superpower! God is within me. God hears me. God gives me self-control.

Prayer is my superpower! God is within me. God hears me. God gives me confidence.

CONCLUSION

Jackson discovered the incredible superpower of prayer within himself and the life-changing impact it has when activated. At school and at home, when faced with moments of fear, frustration, and anger, prayer became his way to victory.

Through his journey, Jackson has learned that no matter how tough life gets as a black boy or how others may treat him, God hears every prayer.

In your hardest moments—when it feels like no one understands—

find your quiet space and talk to God. He's always waiting to listen. As you grow in this power, remember to share it with others and use it for good.

Whatever challenges come your way, do not allow your young age, skin color, family situation, or financial circumstance keep you from discovering and activating your superpower. Trust that prayer will give you the strength to overcome. You are deeply loved by God, and He's with you every step of the way.

ABOUT THE AUTHOR

Zaccheus L. Moss grew up in the small town of Jackson, Alabama, raised by his mother, an educator whose values shaped every phase of his life. Those areas include faith, family, and business.

Zaccheus received a Bachelor

of Science in Business Administration from Alabama State University in 1998.

After working for several Fortune 500 companies, in 2005, Zaccheus moved to Greenville, South Carolina, where he began his career with Norfolk Southern and was blessed to be introduced to his wife, Layna Robinson, Moss whom he has been married to since 2008.

During his time in Greenville, Moss volunteered in several organizations as part of his family's legacy in ministry.

Licensed as a minister under his spiritual covering, Apostle Bertha Terry, he was later licensed under the leadership of Bishop Johnathan Alvarado of Grace Church International in Atlanta.

In 2019, Moss self-published Prayers for Education: Welcoming God Back to Schools, a book that is a collection of prayers for students, parents, and teachers to pray.

In Moss' heart, families praying together is a critical ingredient in family success and survival in times such as this.

Connect With Moss:

Email: businessaggie@gmail.com

Instagram: @businessaggie

Facebook: @Zaccheus L. Moss

Phone: 864-414-9886